MANY THOUSAND GONE

MANY THOUSAND GONE

African Americans from Slavery to Freedom

•

BY VIRGINIA HAMILTON

•

ILLUSTRATED BY LEO AND DIANE DILLON

•

Alfred A. Knopf   *New York*

To the progenitor:

Grandfather Levi Perry,
who led the way North to Freedom
and told the tale.
Pass it on.

V. H.

To those still
fighting the good fight

L. D. *&* D. D.

THIS IS A BORZOI BOOK
PUBLISHED BY ALFRED A. KNOPF

Text copyright © 1993 by Virginia Hamilton
Illustrations copyright © 1993 by Leo and Diane Dillon

All rights reserved under International and Pan-American Copyright
Conventions. Published in the United States by Alfred A. Knopf,
a division of Random House, Inc.,
New York, and simultaneously in Canada by Random House of Canada
Limited, Toronto. Distributed by Random House, Inc., New York.
Designed by Jane Byers Bierhorst.

Originally published in hardcover as a Borzoi Book by
Alfred A. Knopf, in 1993.
First paperback edition: January 1996

Library of Congress Cataloging-in-Publication Data
Hamilton, Virginia. Many Thousand Gone:
African Americans from Slavery to Freedom
by Virginia Hamilton : pictures by Leo and Diane Dillon.
p.   cm.
Summary: Recounts the journey of Black slaves to
freedom via the underground railroad, an extended group of
people who helped fugitive slaves in many ways.
1. Underground railroad—Juvenile literature.
2. Fugitive slaves—United States—Juvenile literature.
[1. Underground railroad. 2. Fugitive slaves.]
I. Dillon, Leo, ill.   II. Dillon, Diane, ill.   III. Title.
E450.H23   1993   89-19988   973.7'115—dc20

ISBN 0-394-92873-3 (lib. bdg.)   ISBN 0-679-87936-6 (pbk.)
Printed in the United States of America

10 9 8 7 6

Contents

PART THREE · EXODUS TO FREEDOM

MANY THOUSAND GONE

Part One

SLAVERY
IN AMERICA

The system of human slavery came to the English colony of Virginia in America in 1619. It was August; a Dutch ship, a "man of warre," traded the colony at Jamestown, Virginia, "twenty Negars." The twenty were Africans stolen from their homes by slave traders. They were traded to the Virginia colony in exchange for food and other supplies. This trade in human beings took place one year before the *Mayflower* landed the Pilgrims at Plymouth, Massachusetts.

The Africans were made indentured servants (giving service for a stated length of time, usually seven years) to the planters or farmers who had traded for them.

There were also white and Native American indentured servants in Jamestown. And, like the Africans, they received no wages. They were bound to their owners just as slaves were to masters.

Indentured servants grew to hate their lives and began to run away. The Native American indentured servants knew the countryside. They would vanish within the forests and find their way back to their own communities, often taking the former Africans and the white servants with them. This caused grave problems for the colonists. And it wasn't long before they adopted regulations governing the institution of servitude.

For example, in Virginia, the ever-increasing number of black servants were forbidden to have arms and ammunition. By 1660, Virginia and Maryland had made the black servants slaves for life. A child born of a slave mother inherited her status. If the mother had bought her freedom, the child was born free.

It is difficult to believe, but throughout the plantation period there were free blacks as well as slaves in the South. Their position was always unstable and dangerous, for at any time they could be sold back into bondage. The white slave owners hated and feared freed blacks, whom they believed set a bad example for their slaves.

In the last twenty-five years of the seventeenth century the slave trade grew by leaps and bounds. Hundreds of ships went to Africa from Europe and England to barter in human beings. And nearly 50,000 Africans were shipped to America as slaves.

Somersett

In 1669, a slave known as Somersett traveled from Boston, Massachusetts, to England with his owner, a man called Stewart. They settled in London. Two years later, Somersett ran away. He was soon caught by Stewart. But Stewart no longer wanted Somersett; the slave seemed to have contracted the dreaded "running-away disease," drapetomania. (At the time, drapetomania was actually thought to be an illness!) So Stewart put Somersett on a ship bound for Jamaica, where he would be sold as a slave.

Before the ship could sail, a religious group known as Quakers obtained a writ of habeas corpus and served it on the ship's captain.

The writ, or order, was a protection against unlawful imprisonment. It barred the slave owner from taking action against Somersett until the captain went before a judge or court.

At the hearing, the judge said that in England, slavery could exist only by what was called *positive law,* law that had been set by the government. Since there was no such law in England, a man's freedom could not be taken away from him on the grounds that he was a slave. Therefore, said the judge, Somersett could go free.

The Somersett decision was the final and most famous in a series of legal decisions declaring that any black person entering England was free. The British slave trade ended in 1807. It was abolished throughout the British Empire in 1833.

Quaker Protest

In 1688, the religious body of Quakers, also known as the Society of Friends, formally protested the American slave system. A group of Friends in Germantown, Pennsylvania, published an antislavery resolution. It has been called the earliest known religious protest against slavery and the traffic in "men-body."

Now, though they are black, we cannot conceive there is more liberty to have them slaves, as it is to have other white ones. There is a saying, that we should do to all men like as we will be done to ourselves; making no difference of what generation, descent, or colour they are.

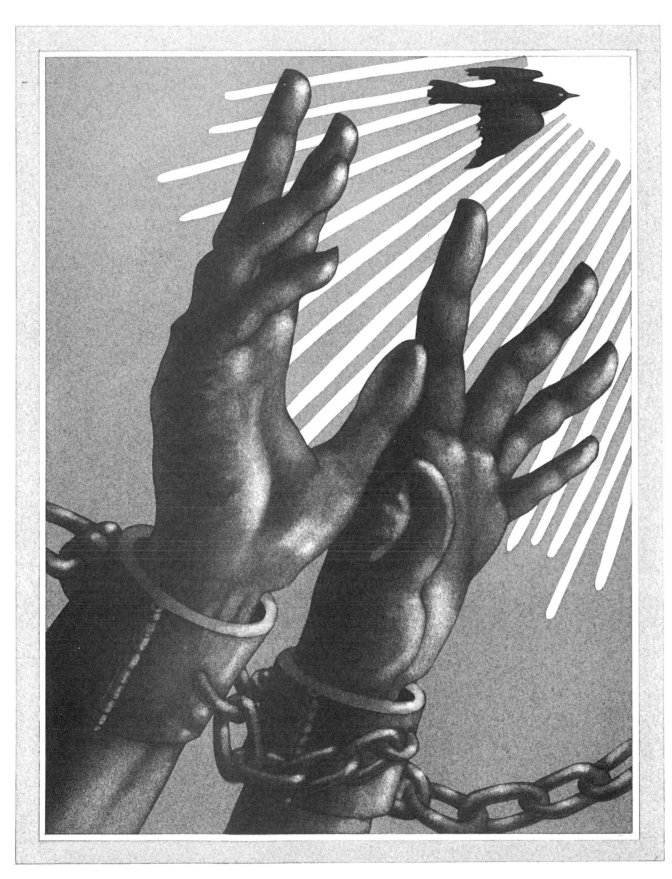

And those who steal or rob men, and those who buy or purchase them, are they not all alike? Here is liberty of conscience, which is right and reasonable; here ought to be likewise liberty of the body. . . . But to bring men hither, or to rob and sell them against their will, we are against.

A Prince

Ukawsaw Gronniosaw was born a prince in 1710 in the kingdom of Bornu (now in northeastern Nigeria), southwest of Lake Chad. His mother was the eldest daughter of the reigning king. Prince Ukawsaw lived well and was doted upon by his mother and father. He wore necklaces of gold and ivory and chains of gold on his ankles and wrists. The glowing jewelry was the emblem of his status and princely privilege.

Ukawsaw had six brothers and sisters who all thought him rather odd, for he often asked questions of his family that were impossible to answer. He would raise his hands to the sky, asking his mother who it was that lived up there. His mother said there were the sun, moon, and stars above and nothing else. The answer made Ukawsaw very unhappy. He was sure there was some power even greater than the sun, moon, and stars, which his family worshiped.

Once, after a violent storm with sweeping black clouds and crashing thunder, Ukawsaw said, "My dear Mother, pray tell me who is the great Man of Power that makes the thunder?"

Again, his mother told him there was no power but that of the sun, moon, and stars. These shining lights and no other had made their world.

"But how did all the people come here?" asked Ukawsaw.

"They came from one another," she answered, taking the prince back many generations.

"But who made the *first man* and who made the first cow, the first lion, and where does the fly come from, as no one can make *him?*"

His mother became very upset. She feared that her son had gone mad. She told his father about his questions. The father became quite angry. He would punish Ukawsaw severely, he said, if he ever asked such questions again.

The prince never again spoke to his mother on the subject of the Man of Power above. But he was deeply unhappy. He no longer rode the goats, which was a custom of the country; goat riding had always been his pleasure. He no longer shot his bow. He found no satisfaction in any of his former pleasures. Both his father and mother hated seeing him so miserable.

When Ukawsaw was fifteen, in 1725, a merchant came from the Gold Coast, from Guinea, in western Africa. He often traded with the inhabitants of Ukawsaw's province. This time he took notice of

Ukawsaw. After inquiring about his unhappiness, the merchant convinced Ukawsaw's parents to allow the prince to go home with him for a visit. He had sons of his own, said the merchant, and they would make good companions for Ukawsaw.

The merchant said the prince would get to "see the houses with wings. And see them walk upon the water!"

Ukawsaw was astonished by the idea of winged houses. He was even more surprised when the merchant said, "Come see the *white folks.*" The merchant told Ukawsaw's mother that he would bring her son back after he had shown him the sights.

So Ukawsaw's parents agreed. Perhaps this journey would take away their son's sadness and bring him back sensible and happy.

Ukawsaw's mother decided to go with him to the edge of their territory, for she wouldn't allow him to travel so far away without family company at least part of the way.

They set out across the desert in the caravan of the merchant. They rode camels. Ukawsaw's mother stayed with them for the first three hundred miles. Then, convinced that her son was in safe hands, she turned back.

Ukawsaw found the trip very exciting. As soon as night fell, the stillness was split open by the roar of lions. The caravan made a circle of fire, keeping camels, men, and equipment well within the fire ring.

Each daybreak, the caravan would start up again. Always there was something unusual to see. Ukawsaw looked on with awe as they passed through a valley of marble surrounded by high mountains. There were many colors of marble, and veins of gold ran through it. The sight of the vast place stayed in Ukawsaw's thoughts long after the caravan had left it behind.

As the trip continued, Ukawsaw found that he was not completely among friends. The merchant's partner had joined the caravan and wanted to get rid of Ukawsaw. There were difficulties in having him along, he said, though he never made it clear what trouble he foresaw. But when the caravan came to a river, the partner tried to get the merchant to have Ukawsaw drowned. The merchant wouldn't hear of such a thing.

For the remainder of the journey, Prince Ukawsaw feared to sleep or let down his guard in any way. But finally, after an overland trip of a thousand miles, they reached the coast and the merchant's home. Drums beat a welcome and horns blew long and loud in tribute to the prince, the grandson of the king of Bornu. Ukawsaw was pleased by this show of respect arranged by the merchant and felt much relieved.

But by evening everything changed again. Two of the merchant's sons came to see Ukawsaw. "Tomorrow you are to die!" they told him. Their own king, they said, would have him beheaded.

"It's not true," exclaimed Ukawsaw. "I came here to play with you and to see the winged houses walk upon the water!"

"Your father sent you only to spy," they replied. "When you went back home, you would know things about our country and your father would make war on us and win. That is why you will never go home. You will have your head cut off!"

Prince Ukawsaw's heart sank as his fear rose. Then he was locked up. He thought of escaping, but wondered where he would go. He was so far from home, and without a friend.

But then the king himself had a change of heart. Rather than have him killed, the king returned him to the merchant. The merchant in turn sold Prince Ukawsaw to a Dutch sea captain for two yards of checked cloth.

The merchant took Ukawsaw's gold wristbands, necklaces, and bracelets before he sent him away with the sea captain, who spoke a language Ukawsaw couldn't understand.

However, Ukawsaw did understand the chains that now bound his hands and ankles. All heavy chains. And there was a thick one around his neck. Ukawsaw knew now that he could not go unless the captain said for him to go. He could do nothing with his hands tied; he was no longer free. He was a slave.

Now he knew who and what were white folks. Besides the captain, they were the men with white skin and light-colored hair who ran the houses with wings, which he discovered were sailing ships. They were grand and immense as they climbed up and slid down the waves of the sea.

Ukawsaw spent a long time on a great water. The wing sails of the house ship ballooned against the wind. The vessel moved swiftly on the sea. It was a terrible time for Ukawsaw and the others who were slaves and chained belowdecks without fresh air. Once a day water was thrown over them. They were forced to keep their mouths open for most of the drenching. In that way, Ukawsaw and the others could drink and keep alive.

Then came another long time and, finally, a stop at Barbados, in the British West Indies. Ukawsaw, weak and weary, was taken off the ship. He was sold at auction for $50 to a New York man named Van Horn.

Prince Ukawsaw Gronniosaw's life continued in slavery for many years. During that time he learned about God and heaven, the great "Man of Power" above he had searched for all of his life. And he became quite religious.

Life was difficult but life went on. Eventually, Ukawsaw went to England and became free. He married and raised a family. Now called James Albert, he began to write about his sad life: "As poor pilgrims, we are travelling through many difficulties, waiting for the call, when the Lord shall deliver us out of the evils of this world . . ."

His autobiography was published in Bath, England, in 1770, when he was sixty years old. It is titled *A Narrative of the Most Remarkable Particulars in the Life of James Albert Ukawsaw Gronniosaw, an African Prince—Related by Himself.*

The Gronniosaw narrative is very rare and is one of the few such sources that have been preserved.

A Vanished Slave and His Return

In 1750, William Brown, of Framingham, Massachusetts, put this notice about his missing "property"—a slave—in the *Boston Gazette:*

Short, curly hair, his knees more nearly together than common; had on . . . new buckskin breeches, blue yarn stockings and checked woolen shirt. Whoever shall take up said runaway, and convey him to above said master, shall receive ten pounds . . . And all masters of [slaves] or others, are hereby cautioned against concealing or carrying off said servant on penalty of law.

Owner Brown's slave disappeared so completely that it was thought he must have gone to sea. Nothing was heard about him for twenty years. But on the evening of March 5, 1770, the escaped slave, whose name was Crispus Attucks, turned up on Dock Square in Boston.

At this time there were many reports of skirmishes between colonial citizens and the British troops who protected Great Britain's interests in America. Attucks, who lived near the square, had heard that a British soldier had beaten a young American boy with his musket. Full of revolutionary zeal, Attucks urged the crowd in the square to help him get rid of the British soldier. Some in the crowd were sailors carrying sticks. And Attucks led them to the custom house on King Street. Menacingly, they moved on the sentry in his box. Just then, seven British soldiers arrived, commanded by Captain Thomas Preston.

"Don't be afraid!" Crispus Attucks shouted. "They dare not fire."

He and the crowd stood their ground. Then someone hurled a stick at a soldier. The soldier raised his musket and fired, hitting Attucks in the chest. Attucks fell and the crowd surged forward. More shots rang out and another citizen fell to the ground. In all, five men fell, and not one of them was a British soldier.

Crispus Attucks, free from bondage all these many years, now lay dead, the victim of what later became known as the Boston Massacre. He was the first martyr of the war that would come—the American Revolution.

A Kidnapped Child

Olaudah Equiana was born in Benin, Nigeria, in 1745. At the age of eleven he was kidnapped from his home and sold to slave traders along the Nigerian coast. From there he was taken on a slave ship bound for Barbados, in the West Indies. Years later, Equiana would write about his time on that ship:

I was soon put down under the decks and was greeted by such a stench as I had never experienced in my life. I became so sick and low that I was not able to eat, nor had I the least desire to taste anything.

Soon, to my grief, two of the white men offered me eatables and, on my refusing to eat, one of them held me fast by the hands, and laid me across, I think, the windlass, and tied my feet, while the other flogged me severely.

I had never experienced anything of this kind before . . . (and) in a little time after, amongst the poor chained men, I found some of my own nation . . . I feared I should be put to death, the white people looked and acted, as I thought, in so savage a manner. I asked my countrymen if these white people had no country, but lived in this hollow place [the ship]? They told me that they did not, but came from a distant one.

"Then how comes it in all our country we never heard of them!" I asked. They told me because they lived so very far off . . .

I asked how the vessel could go? They told me they could not tell; but that there were cloths put upon masts by the help of the ropes I saw, and then the vessel went on . . .

Equiana described the misery and death belowdecks and the despair and suicide abovedecks among the wretched prisoners. Being strong, he survived the terrifying Middle Passage, which claimed the lives of so many thousands of kidnapped Africans.

After reaching America, Equiana was sold to a Captain Pascal, commander of the ship *The Industrious Bee*. Captain Pascal renamed him Gustavus Vassa and sent him to England, where Vassa became the servant for two devout women. They taught him to read the Bible. In this way he was able to continue his education in the English language, which had begun on *The Industrious Bee*.

Vassa was sold and resold. He went to sea and was shipped to the West Indies. He was bought by a Philadelphia merchant, a Quaker,

and was treated with kindness. He was allowed to earn money and pay for his freedom.

Once free, Gustavus Vassa returned to England, where he worked to end slavery, petitioning the British Parliament for its abolition. His autobiography, *The Interesting Narrative of the Life of Olaudah Equiana, or Gustavus Vassa,* was published with great success in London in 1789.

Many Africans like Vassa were captured and brought to the coast of Africa by black or Arab slave traders. There they were sold to white slave traders for goods, spices, and rum. It was not unusual to find children, as well as adults, in chains on the slave ships.

Aboard ship, none of the captured Africans took their enslavement lightly. Some fought back and were killed and thrown overboard. Others, forced by the low ship ceilings to sit in a crouch for the eight- to ten-week voyage, died by the hundreds. Thirty percent of them did not survive the Middle Passage across the ocean from Africa to America. Still others attempted to drown themselves as soon as the ship docked.

Survivors burned with hatred of the chains that bound them and of those who had carried them away. They grieved, crying for their homelands and families and all they had known and loved.

Jenny Slew

By 1770, nearly a half million slaves were part of the population of the American South. Alarmed at the growing numbers, Virginians petitioned the British king to stop the slave trade into America, stating that the bringing of slaves into the colonies "hath long been considered as a trade of great inhumanity . . ."

The ferment over equality and liberty in the pre-Revolutionary War period caused many individuals to make a public outcry against slavery. How could citizens plead for freedom for themselves, many asked, when there were those among them still enslaved?

Jenny Slew was called a mulatto, the name for a person having

one white and one black parent. In 1766, she went to court in the Massachusetts colony, accusing citizen John Whipple of capturing her "with force and arms" four years earlier. Whipple, she said, had "held and kept her in servitude . . . without any lawful right and authority" until March 1766. She asked twenty-five British pounds as damages.

At first, John Whipple tried proving there was no such person as Jenny Slew. When that didn't work, he pleaded not guilty to her complaint. The court decided in Whipple's favor. He received a judgment of four pounds.

Jenny Slew then took her case to the Superior Court in Salem, Massachusetts. There a jury reversed the judgment, deciding in her favor. She was awarded four pounds and court costs.

PART TWO

RUNNING-AWAYS

The Religious Society of Friends had branched out from England to the American colonies. These Quakers believed strongly that slavery should be abolished, and they were among the first whites to help the running-aways, as escaping slaves were often called. They formed an important core group along with black freemen and freewomen and running-aways in the abolition movement. They were also a significant part of the escape network first known as the underground road (later called the Underground Railroad), which operated before and during the American Revolution and throughout the 1800s.

The underground road was neither a road nor underground. It was any number of houses, caves, hay mounds, root cellars, attics, high branches of trees, chimneys, hidden rooms, and empty barns— any place a running-away could hide. It was also all the paths and trails leading to such places.

The first guides along the road were black slaves. Resisting their owners, they secretly led running-aways from one plantation to the next—and eventually out of the South. Occasionally, these black movers would get angry and feel hopeless; then they would slip away for a time, into the great forests. Often, they became lost and only barely managed to find their way back to the plantations. There they suffered punishment—whippings, or worse. Sometimes they saw no other way than to run themselves.

Free blacks, always in danger of being forced into bondage, also kept close watch on the road. They often handed running slaves over to Quakers. Some of these Quakers in the South had owned slaves, as had the Friend who had owned Gustavus Vassa. Others were so uncomfortable owning human property that they allowed their slaves to buy their freedom. There were Southern Quakers who would even purchase slaves in order to set them free.

Fugitives running out of the slave South to the free North seldom told anyone who they were. The slave owner hunting them might have posted their names and their descriptions. So the less "identity" they had, the better their chances of escaping.

There were ten to twenty miles between each underground stop. A Friend might lead a fugitive from one stop to the next, to a house, perhaps. The Friend would knock. A question was called out from behind the closed door: "Who's there?"

Came the reply: "A Friend, with a friend." That meant a Quaker and his or her running-away charge were at the door.

The password having been given, the door was opened and yet another fugitive became invisible along the line to the North.

Information was passed along by the "underground telegraph"— that is, by word of mouth or by mail from one conductor to the next. Messages were always in code: "Dear Grinnel—Uncle Tom says if the roads are not too bad, you can look for those fleeces of wool by tomorrow. Send them on to test the market and price, no back charges . . ." In other words, some running-away slaves could be expected in the morning, and Grinnel should send them farther along the underground road.

Running-aways considered themselves free once they had crossed the north shore of the Ohio River. They understood they were free, but not safe. There were still dangers—bounty hunters and proslavery settlers, who might capture a fugitive for the reward posted by the slave owner.

Southerners called the running-aways maroons, wild ones, or desperadoes. Every day they were free was a reminder to other slaves that escape was possible. Nothing except a slave uprising upset the slaveholder more than the thought of a maroon stalking his plantation, bent on leading others to freedom. Maroons were hunted relentlessly.

In 1793, Eli Whitney invented the cotton engine, or gin, as it was called. While one slave might process a pound of cotton a day, a cotton gin could process a thousand pounds a day. Thus, far more cotton could be turned into cloth. Cotton became the king of commodities as the textile industry boomed in the South. With the need for more field hands to pick cotton to feed the cotton gins, the demand for black slave labor rose dramatically.

It can be no accident that the first Fugitive Slave Act was passed that same year. The act made it a crime to shelter a slave or to prevent his or her arrest. If the slave owner or his agent caught a running-away he owned in a free state, the law allowed the owner to forcibly bring the slave back into slavery.

Elizabeth Freeman

There were not many slaves in Massachusetts in the late 1700s. And those who were slaves were apparently treated with some decency. Many took their meals with their white owners; few were sold away.

Incidents of cruelty did occur, though. Elizabeth Freeman, known as Mom Bett, and her sister worked in the same Massachusetts household. One day, the mistress became angry at Mom Bett's sister and tried to strike her with a hot poker. Mom Bett was in the way and the poker struck her by mistake. She suffered a searing burn on the arm.

Mom Bett left the house almost immediately. She would not go back, even though the mistress begged her to. "I'll never go back," Mom Bett said, and she never did. But she did carry the scar from the hot poker for the rest of her life.

The owner tried to get Mom Bett back by going to court. But the Massachusetts Bill of Rights, recently adopted, stated that "all men [meaning all people] are born free and equal," and the court decided in Mom Bett's favor. Now officially free, she began working as a servant, then became a midwife. She lived to be ninety-seven or ninety-eight.

Mom Bett's case was one of the first to test the Massachusetts Bill of Rights.

The Right of Chloe

In 1792, Chloe Cooley was the property of a man called Vrooman, who lived in Queenstown, Canada (now Queenston, Ontario). That summer Chloe learned, to her horror, that Vrooman had sold her to an American. She knew nothing about America or her new owner, only that she would be taken to him by boat. She was so terrified that she had to be bound and carried onto the boat lest she run away.

When the boat docked on the American shore, where her new owner waited, Chloe was carried off, screaming and struggling. She fought as best she could, but still she was taken away.

Of course, Chloe's owner had every *legal* right over her. He could

rope, sell, and export her just as he would one of his farm animals. She was his property according to the law, without a single right of her own. But many Canadians thought Vrooman had treated her cruelly by selling her away.

The Executive Council of Ontario was so disturbed by the incident that a hearing was held to discuss it. The Executive Council then passed a resolution "to prevent the continuance of such violent breaches of the Public Peace . . . and that his Majesty's Attorney General be . . . directed to prosecute the said Vrooman."

The Chloe Cooley incident resulted in the Imperial Act of 1793, which outlawed the importation of slaves into Upper Canada.

Advertisements

The two announcements below appeared in *The York Gazette and Oracle* in February 1800 and September 1803. They were placed by the Honorable Peter Russell, government administrator of the province of York in Upper Canada, who was also a slave owner. The "advertisements" give a glimpse into the mind of a slaver and into the life of a black woman, formerly his property.

1800

To be sold, a Black Woman named Peggy, age 40 years, and a Black Boy her son named Jupiter, age 15 years. Both of them the property of the subscriber [Russell]. The woman is a tolerable cook and washerwoman and perfectly understands making soap and candles . . . price . . . $150. For the boy $200, payable in three years with interest from the day of sale and to be secured by bond, etc. But one-fourth less will be taken for ready money.

1803

The subscriber's Black servant, Peggy, not having his permission to absent herself from his service, the public are hereby cautioned from employing or harbouring her without the owner's leave. Whoever will do so after this notice . . . expect to be treated as the law directs.

The Gabriel Prosser Uprising

From the very beginning, the institution of human bondage resulted in slave revolts and uprisings. As the importation of slaves to America increased, so too did the slaves' desperate longing to be free. Early on, slaves realized that running away was a painful and slow process, freeing one slave at a time. But uprisings could set numbers of them free all at once.

The Prosser insurrection took place in 1800, following two serious, yet poorly organized, uprisings—one in Stono, South Carolina, in 1739 and the other in New York City in 1741. Gabriel Prosser's revolt was a model of planning and organization.

Six feet two inches tall, the slave property of Thomas Prosser, of Virginia, Gabriel was twenty-four years old in the spring of 1800. He had two brothers, Solomon and Martin, and a wife, Nanny. For some time, the four had been making secret preparations. They had also persuaded other slaves to follow them.

Gabriel Prosser knew much about military planning and war. He was an admirer of a black man from Haiti named Pierre Dominique Toussaint L'Ouverture (pronounced Too-SAWNT Leh-ove-TUWR). Toussaint L'Ouverture was the leader of the Haitian revolution in 1791, which began when 100,000 Haitian slaves went on a rampage, killing slave owners and burning down plantations. L'Ouverture seized control of the revolt and turned frenzied slaves into a disciplined army.

Gabriel Prosser believed he could do what L'Ouverture had done: He would start an army and overcome the cruel white men who kept black people as slaves.

Whenever possible, Gabriel, his brothers, and his wife slipped away from their labor to discuss strategy. They also managed to find storehouses of government ammunition in Richmond, Virginia.

By the late summer of 1800, Gabriel had brought together several thousand slaves who swore they would help him overthrow the slave owners to create a black stronghold in Virginia.

The Prosser plan was to attack Richmond with three columns of men. The first prong would take the storehouse and claim all the guns. Another prong would liberate the powder store. The last prong would overcome the town itself, striking every person who was white, except for French people, Methodists, Quakers, and the poor. The French would be spared because they had taught freedom lovers the phrase "Liberty, Equality, Fraternity"; the Methodists and Quakers, because they believed in liberty; and the poor whites because, in a slave society, they suffered almost as much as the slaves.

With the element of surprise, the plan might have worked. But on the night marked for the uprising, August 30, there was a terrible storm. Rain poured; the land flooded. Bridges and roads were washed away. Nothing could move in such violent weather. Far worse was the fact that two slaves betrayed Gabriel Prosser and revealed his plan to a slave owner.

Unknown to Prosser, the governor called out the militia. Before Prosser could bring his men together after the storm, the militia attacked.

Gabriel Prosser was captured on board a ship as he tried to escape. He would not reveal his plan of insurrection. His captors were amazed by his proud, unflinching manner. He knew he would be put to death and said not a word about the uprising he had led. He was tried, convicted, and hanged on October 7, 1800. Thirty-five of his co-conspirators were also hanged.

The uprising terrified whites everywhere, including those in the North, and resulted in a wave of legislation limiting the freedom of all black people. In 1804, Ohio passed a series of slave codes (called Black Laws or Black Codes) that limited the movement and the rights of free blacks. Many other Northern states also passed Black Codes. Black settlers were barred from the Oregon territory and from Indiana and Illinois.

In 1822, a South Carolina slave named Denmark Vesey planned an uprising. It was betrayed, and 130 blacks were arrested, along with four whites. The whites were convicted of being in sympathy with the plot and were fined and jailed. Denmark Vesey, five of his aides, and

thirty-one others were hanged. The slave informer of the plot was given his freedom by the state and $50 a year, increased to $200 in 1857.

Josiah Henson,
Running-away and Guide

Josiah (Si) Henson was born in the slave state of Maryland. His father had been whipped one hundred lashes for trying to protect Josiah's mother from an overseer. With his ear nailed to the whipping post, the father took the harsh punishment. Afterward, his ear was cut off.

Henson's father was sold to the deep South, somewhere in Alabama, and neither Josiah nor his mother ever heard of him again.

Josiah himself was sold and resold many times from the age of six. As a youth, he was beaten so badly by an overseer that for the rest of his life he could not raise his arms as high as his head. As a man, he wrote about the beating:

It was five months before I could work at all. And the first time I tried to plough, a hard knock of the colter [a sharp blade attached to the plow] against a stone shattered my shoulderblades again, and gave me even greater agony than at first. And so I have gone through life maimed and mutilated . . . the free vigorous play of muscle and arm was gone forever.

Si Henson finally escaped through Indiana and the Ohio wilderness with his sick wife and children. Half dead from starvation and chased by wolves, the family was helped along by northern Ohio Native Americans. Eventually, the Hensons reached Canada.

"It was the 28th of October, 1830," wrote Henson, "in the morning, when my feet first touched the Canada shore. I threw myself on the ground, rolled in the sand, seized handfuls of it and kissed them, and danced round till, in the eyes of several who were present, I passed for a madman.

" 'He's some crazy fellow,' said a Colonel Warren, who happened to be there."

"Oh, no . . . don't you know? I'm free!" Si told him.

The colonel burst out laughing. "Well, I never knew freedom to make a man roll in the sand . . ." he said.

It wasn't long before Josiah and his wife began helping other blacks in Canada, who found the cold climate almost impossible to deal with. Si taught them how to care for themselves in the winter and, later, how to grow their crops and how to use the money they made.

One of the people he helped was James Lightfoot. Lightfoot was

fearful of going back for his family in Maysville, Kentucky, since it was behind the slavery wall. Si Henson said he would go, and he did. He *walked* four hundred miles through New York, Pennsylvania, and Ohio to Kentucky. Only then did he discover that the Lightfoot family in Kentucky was too afraid to make the long trek back to Canada.

Henson heard about another group, fifty miles away, willing to run. At once, he set out to find them, which he did. He then acted as their guide through the North. There was an unusually large number of them—thirty—from various Southern states. Bringing them out as a group, Si Henson crossed the Ohio River with them and went on up through Cincinnati. He took the underground road through the Quaker town of Richmond, Indiana, and on to Canada.

A year later, Henson went back for the Lightfoot family. This time they were willing to follow him. Though slave hunters pursued them as far as Lake Erie, they made a successful escape and journeyed on to Canada.

Josiah Henson sailed to England and was the first fugitive slave given an audience with Queen Victoria. He went on to become a Methodist minister and a prominent abolitionist.

A Slave

The underground road was named for the deed of an actual man born a slave who one day ran away from slavery. It became the name given to all the secret trails that led north, and to the system of human helpers of all races—who braved prison and even death to lead the running-aways to freedom.

Tice Davids inspired the first use of the term "underground road." On a day in 1831 that seemed ordinary, full of pain and hard work for him, Davids discovered that he had changed. He wondered how it had happened that on this day he could not bear to be a slave a moment longer.

It was time for him to make his way north. And so he ran.

Tice knew where he was going. There were Friends across the Ohio River, waiting. North would be somewhere there, and on and on. Word of that had come to him on the plantation. Whispers about liberty had made their way through the servants' quarters and on to the fields. They spread on the wind down to the riverbank. Tice had an idea of what it was to be free. It meant that he might rest without fear covering him like a blanket as he slept. It meant that nobody could buy or sell him.

Not all those who were slaves had the daring to escape. It wasn't that Tice was without fear. But, like others before him, given the chance, he'd take it.

There were those, black and free, who combed the river-bank, looking to help the running-aways. And there were certain Presbyterian ministers from the South who had formed a new church and had settled in the counties of southern Ohio. They were known to be friends of slaves. Like ever-present eagles with fierce, keen eyes, they too watched the great river for the running-aways.

Trusted to be a good servant, Tice had taken his life into his own hands and had run. And now he hurried, running.

"Look for the lantern!" That had been the urgent message passed along the slave quarters for those who would run at night.

"Listen for the bell!" Word was that the lone, distant sound of a bell clanging could be heard from across the wide river—when the wind was right. Other times, the bell seemed to clang up and down the shore. The river might be covered in fog. And hidden deep in the mist on the shore, a running-away could clearly hear the bell. He could follow its ringing all the way over and to a safe house.

Tice Davids would have to find a way across the great water if he was ever to be free. With luck he might find a usable boat or raft along the shore. What would he do if there was nothing to ride across on?

Capture for him was unthinkable, and he kept on running.

"Heard tell that on the other side, a slave is no longer such. They say that on the other side of the wide water, a slave is a free man."

That was the word and the truth that all Kentucky slaves believed. He kept that in mind as he ran. He looked back, knowing what he would see. There were the planter and his men, coming after him. The slave owner. Some called him master; Tice wouldn't when he could avoid it.

Friends, waiting across the river, was the word he could count on. If only he could get to the Friends!

He had been running for some time. Almost as though he were dreaming, he lifted one leg and then the other. Whatever had possessed him to try to break out?

Now he was at the Kentucky shore and it was empty. There was no boat to row, no raft to pole. The distant Ohio shore seemed farther than far. There was nothing for it but to swim.

Tice waded into the water, tired out before he began. The cold wet of the river shocked him, revived him. He knew to calm himself down and soon got his mind in hand. He began moving his arms, swimming in clean, long strokes.

About halfway across, Tice thought he heard a bell. The sound gave him strength and he swam gamely on.

It took the slave owner time to locate a skiff, but a small boat was found at last. He and his men shoved off and gave chase. The slave owner never let his slave out of his sight. Even when Tice staggered from the water onto the Ohio shore, the owner glared through the mist and pinpointed the dark, exhausted figure.

"Think we have him now," he said. He blinked to get the wet from his eyes. It was one blink too many. Tice Davids was gone. Disappeared!

"It's not believable," the owner said. "I saw him before my eyes and now he's gone. Vanished! It's not possible, but there it is."

The slave owner searched the shore every which way. He looked into ditches. He and his men beat the bushes and crept into caves and gazed up into trees. They poked the haystacks in the fields. They talked to people in the slavery-hating settlement at Ripley, Ohio, and they had their suspicions. But not one of the townsfolk would admit to having seen anybody running away. The Kentucky slave owner never again saw Tice Davids.

"Well, I'm going home," he said finally. He and his men crossed the river again and returned to Kentucky.

"Only one way to look at it," he told everyone at home, shaking his head in disbelief. "Tice must've gone on an underground road!"

Tice Davids made his way north through all of Ohio, all the way to Sandusky, on Lake Erie. There, at last, he settled, a free man—and the first to travel the underground road.

Later, the underground road took on an inspiring new name in honor of the amazing steam trains on parallel rails then coming into their own in America: *the Underground Railroad!*

Those who guided the running-aways along the highly secret system of the Underground Railroad had the cleverness to call themselves "conductors," the name used on the steam railway trains. The

safe houses and secret hiding places known to the conductors were called "stations" and "depots," after railway stations and railway depots. Eventually, Tice Davids became a conductor on the Underground Railroad, helping other running-aways escape.

The Nat Turner Rebellion

Nat Turner was born the year of the Gabriel Prosser uprising, 1800. The rebellion he led is the most well known of the major slave revolts. Turner died in 1831, the year Tice Davids vanished on the underground road.

Abolitionist William Lloyd Garrison founded his antislavery newspaper *The Liberator* in the same year, 1831. Garrison became the paper's editor, demanding freedom at once for blacks in bondage. He wrote that if the South feared more insurrections like Nat Turner's rebellion, the way to solve its problem was "Immediate Emancipation"—freedom for its slaves.

"That which is not just is not law," wrote Garrison. "Let Southern oppressors tremble," he warned, foreseeing the human rights battles to come. "Let all the enemies of the persecuted blacks tremble."

Nat was born in Southampton County, Virginia, the property of slave owner Benjamin Turner. Nat's mother had been born in Africa. She had an abiding hatred of bondage and did not want her son to live as a slave.

When Nat was three or four, his mother overheard him telling other children something he couldn't have known about, for it had happened before he was born. She knew she hadn't told him, because it was something a parent would not reveal to a child.

When questioned, Nat stuck to his story. He even added details his mother swore he couldn't know. Yet he did.

Other people were called in to hear what Nat told. They too were astonished by his knowledge. They said he would be a prophet when he was a man, since he knew things that had happened before his own birth.

The mark of prophecy followed Nat. Slaves believed he had a mysterious power. He grew into the kind of man who believed God had placed him on earth for some extraordinary reason.

Turner was five and a half feet tall, of dark complexion, erect and strong in appearance. He did not smoke or drink. Other slaves looked on him with pride. He had learned quickly to read. He became deeply religious and a powerful preacher. From his frequent Bible readings, he came to believe that his purpose was to free the slaves. Then he started hearing voices and having visions.

Nat plowed his owner's fields and heard the sound of freedom. He believed in what he heard.

He told other slaves there would be a warring between the races. And in the late part of August 1831, it began.

Nat Turner and his men started murdering slave owners—men, women, and children. Wherever they went to kill, they took away slave recruits to their cause and carried off guns and ammunition.

Turner's band increased to sixty, and his rebellion went on unchecked for forty-eight hours.

The plan was to attack the county seat of Jerusalem, Virginia, for supplies and money. On the way, the Turner band stopped for reinforcements at a nearby plantation. This was a grave mistake, for a patrol was waiting. The unexpected posse sent the Turner band running in every direction. By this time, fifty-five whites had been killed.

Nat concealed himself for the night and hid in the woods for the next couple of days, hoping his men would come to him. But they never did. So he headed for the Great Dismal Swamp, which extended from near Norfolk, Virginia, into North Carolina and was home to a large colony of fugitives. Black children were born and grew up there, spending their whole lives in its stagnant, snake-infested byways. Hunters of slave runaways entered at their peril.

Nat Turner hid in the swamp for weeks, venturing out only at night to fetch water and food.

Meanwhile, the whites sought revenge. They too went out murdering and killed 120 blacks in just one day. These were innocent victims who had nothing to do with Turner's revolt.

White volunteers rode through plantations, running down the slaves. Some slave owners tried to halt the slaughter of the innocent. But nothing could stop the vengeance. Slaves were tortured and burned alive.

More than fifty of Turner's rebels were captured within a few days. They went to trial, but Nat remained at large. All over the South, black people's houses were searched for him and for arms. In response, other revolts led by angry slaves flared in Delaware, Alabama, Kentucky, and Tennessee.

Turner was spotted in a hundred places at once. Thousands of troops searched for him across many states. He managed to remain hidden near the place of his revolt, Southampton County. His home was a cave, until dogs scented his food and he had to run again. Then a farmer found him in a field near one of his haystacks. The farmer shot at him, but Nat got away. Finally, days later, Turner staggered out of hiding, too exhausted to go on. As a prisoner, he told the story of his revolt. It was much like a confession.

"I had a vision," he said, "and I saw white spirits and black spirits engaged in battle, and the sun was darkened—the thunder rolled in the heavens, and blood flowed in streams. And I heard a voice saying, 'Such is your luck, such you are called to see; and let it come rough or smooth, you must surely bear it.'

"I am here loaded with chains," he said finally, "and willing to suffer the fate that awaits me."

Nat Turner was tried on the fifth of November 1831. Twenty of his band were acquitted. Twelve were convicted and removed from the state. Seventeen were hanged, including Nat.

After the hanging, surgeons took Nat's body to dissect it. This man who slaves called the Prophet, who had visions of himself, like Moses, leading his people to freedom, would never know his final humiliation.

It is said that his skin was taken and boiled down for the grease.

Some Conductors on
the Underground Railroad

It was known that Nat Turner had been a preacher and that he could read and write. After his rebellion, slaves were forbidden reading material. The Black Codes were imposed more harshly. Free blacks could not enter the states of Tennessee and Virginia. Black seamen were imprisoned in South Carolina while their ships were in port. It was against the law in North Carolina, Mississippi, and Virginia to distribute antislavery literature.

Increasingly, the only way out for slaves was to run away, even though it meant risking their lives. There were helpers all along the route north, if only the fugitives could find them. Runaways quickly learned that the most trustworthy people in the North were free black conductors on the Railroad.

One such man was John Malvin, a conductor who worked a limited route from one Northern station to the next. He owned a canal boat that ran from Cleveland to Marietta, Ohio, a route that took him close to the Ohio River. His boat carried fugitives.

Another conductor was Leonard Andrew Grimes, the owner of a horse-and-carriage business in Washington, D.C. Using his buggies, Grimes often rescued fugitives. On one rescue he was captured trying to carry away a slave family and then spent two years in prison. Afterward, he went to Boston, where he became the minister of the "fugitive slave church," the Twelfth Baptist Church of Boston. Later, he was involved in one of the most celebrated escaped-slave cases in American history, that of Anthony Burns.

There were hundreds of black conductors in Ohio alone. Because Ohio was just across the river from the slave states of Kentucky and Virginia, it had the most active and numerous Underground Railroad routes.

Jane Lewis was a conductor on the Ohio Underground. From New Lebanon, Ohio, she found her way to the Ohio River and rowed runaways from the far side to the Ohio freedom shore.

Another conductor was Elijah Anderson, known as the "general superintendent" of the northwestern Ohio Underground. He sent 1,000 slaves along the Railroad before he was caught and sent to prison in Kentucky, where he died.

Fugitives from Southern states would risk their lives becoming conductors and going *back* into the South (as did Si Henson) to find their families and other slaves who were willing to run away.

John Mason, a Kentucky runaway, had reached Canada. He became a conductor, going back to his home state and convincing friends to follow him north. After assisting 265 slaves to Canada, he was captured and sold back into slavery. But Mason managed to escape again. It is said that he helped more than 1,000 fugitives along the Underground Railroad.

Two more black men, William Still and Robert Purvis, were famous abolitionists from Philadelphia. Still wrote down the story of every fugitive who passed through his line. While interviewing a runaway from the South in 1850, Still discovered that the fugitive was his own long-lost brother!

Over their lifetimes, Still and Purvis helped some 9,000 fugitives along the Underground Railroad up through Pennsylvania to freedom.

There were white conductors who harbored fugitives also. Some became famous as fierce abolitionist leaders. John Rankin, Levi Coffin, Thomas Garrett, and Elijah Lovejoy, to name a few, lived across the river from slave states. They had no time for arguing the right of their cause. They believed in using force if they had to.

Eliza

There is a runaway slave character called Eliza who escapes from Kentucky over ice floes in the Ohio River in Harriet Beecher Stowe's novel *Uncle Tom's Cabin*. Mrs. Stowe said her book was a "collection and arrangement of real incidents" and that the chase across the ice floes was drawn from an actual rescue involving her husband, Calvin Ellis Stowe, a clergyman, and her brother, Henry Ward Beecher.

The real-life Eliza escaped from Kentucky with her baby in her arms. When she came to the Ohio River, she saw large chunks of ice floating on it. But that didn't stop her, for the slave hunters were in hot pursuit. She leaped from one ice floe to the next in an agonizing act of courage until she reached the freedom shore.

Eliza was rescued by the family of the Reverend John Rankin and stayed in their house above the river. Levi Coffin then aided her on the difficult journey to Canada.

As Eliza left the Rankin Underground station, she told John Rankin that she would come back for her other children, still slaves in Kentucky, in June of the following year. Reverend Rankin doubted that he would ever see her again. But a year later, in June, a man came climbing up to the garden of the Rankin house. It was Eliza, wearing men's clothing, ready to get her children and bring them out.

The Rankins helped her back across the Ohio River into Kentucky. Because it was Sunday, the plantation owner and his wife were away visiting. Eliza hastened to carry off her five children—and two hundred pounds of household goods!

The heavy load slowed them down. By the time they reached the river again, the sun was up and fog on the water was lifting. The Rankins waited for Eliza on the Ohio side, their guns at the ready. They saw dogs and men on horseback spread out on the Kentucky shore. One Rankin son, dressed as a slave woman, slipped across the river. He quickly attracted the slave hunters' attention and led them on a wild-goose chase away from where Eliza and her brood were hidden.

For hours, the slave posse chased the disguised Rankin son. Finally darkness fell and the hunters lost him. A Rankin helper had by then guided Eliza, her family, and all their belongings back across the river to the safe house on the Ohio bluff.

Two weeks later, Eliza and her children were conducted along the Underground Railroad line to Canada.

Isabella, Sojourner

Isabella Baumfree became famous in her lifetime as Sojourner Truth, an abolitionist, lecturer-preacher, and self-styled prophet. She was born in Ulster County, New York, in 1797, the slave of a Dutch owner. And all of her life she would speak with a Dutch accent.

Isabella was sold several times. Her owner refused to free her when all slaves in New York State were freed by the state's Emancipation Act of 1827. Some accounts say she ran away the year before because of beatings by her owner. In any case, she did run to New York City with one of her many children and there found work as a maid. Isabella never learned to read or write. But that didn't stop her from learning or from trying to find a deeper meaning to her life.

When she was forty-six, she felt an urgent desire to come to the aid of her people. "I felt so tall within," she said. "I felt the power of the nation was with me."

It was spring. Deep inside her, Isabella felt she had gone through being born a second time. She knew she must speak out against slavery, and she prepared herself to do just that.

I went to the Lord and asked him to give me a new name. And the Lord gave me Sojourner because I was to travel up and down the land showing the people their sins and being a sign unto them. Afterward I told the Lord I wanted another name 'cause everybody else had two names; and the Lord gave me Truth, because I was to declare the truth to the people.

Now, as she became Sojourner Truth, Isabella felt complete. Six feet tall, thin, with a dark complexion, and very erect, Sojourner Truth set out walking to "gather in my flock." Through the East—Massachusetts, Connecticut—through Ohio, Indiana, Illinois, through Kansas she went, preaching freedom for her people.

She became the most famous and perhaps the best antislavery speaker of her time. Wherever she went, a large crowd gathered to hear her. At first, people were simply curious about this strange black woman. But soon they grew to admire her passion. They thought she had the gift of prophecy. She certainly had a gift for putting words together in a dramatic fashion.

Once she stood up at a meeting to answer someone who had praised the Constitution of the United States. She had the habit of calling everybody children, and she began:

Children, I talk to God and God talks to me. I go and talk to God in the fields and woods. This morning I was walking out, and I got over the fence. I saw the wheat a-holding up its head, looking very big. I go up and take hold of it. You believe it? There was *no* wheat there. I say, "God, what is the matter with this wheat?" And He said to me, "Sojourner, there is a little weevil in it!"

Now I hear talk about the Constitution and the rights of man. I come up and I take hold of this Constitution. It looks mighty big and I feel for my rights but there ain't any there.

Then I say, "God, what ails this Constitution?" He says to me, "Sojourner, there is a little weevil in it!"

Not only did Sojourner Truth address meetings for the abolition-ist cause, she also spoke out for the rights of women:

I've been looking round and watching things, and I know a little mite about women's rights, too . . . I know that it feels a kind of hissing and tickling like to see a colored woman get up again; but we have been long enough trodden down now; we will come up again, and now I am here . . . sitting among you to watch . . . every once in a while I will come out . . . tell you what time of night it is.

At one convention, Sojourner argued against men who thought women needed to be helped into carriages and lifted over ditches. They thought, too, that women had lower intelligence than men and should not vote. She said:

Nobody ever helps me into carriages, or over mud puddles . . . and ain't I a woman? I have ploughed and planted and gathered into barns . . . and ain't I a woman? I could work as much and eat as much as a man . . . and bear the lash as well! And ain't I a woman? I have borne thirteen children, and seen them most all sold off to slavery, and when I cried out with my mother's grief, none but Jesus heard me! And ain't I a woman?

She had a deep voice, like a man's, some said. She was proud in her bearing. Intelligence fairly leaped out of her bright eyes.

Sojourner worked just enough to keep herself going. She slept wherever she could find a place to lie down. There were many attempts to stop her from standing up to lecture at public meetings. But nothing, it seemed, could keep Sojourner down, although she was beaten and even stoned on occasion.

She began wearing a banner across her chest. PROCLAIM LIBERTY THROUGH THE LAND UNTO ALL THE INHABITANTS THEREOF was written across it.

Some people felt threatened by Sojourner's power over crowds. They said there had to be something wrong with her, that maybe she wasn't a female at all!

"Prove you are a woman!" a man demanded once while she was speaking.

Sojourner ripped her blouse open to the waist. Shocked, people turned their eyes away. But it was the heckler's shame, she said, not hers, that she must so prove herself.

When she was old, Sojourner gave up traveling and lecturing. She had taught freedwomen in Washington, D.C., and crusaded for

black settlements on western public lands. And though she was not a part of the Underground Railroad system, she inspired many to travel the secret rails. She lived close by her daughters in Battle Creek, Michigan, and died there at the age of eighty-five, on November 26, 1883. The Sojourner Truth grave is at Oak Hill cemetery in Battle Creek.

The Captain of the *Pearl*

Daniel Drayton, captain of a ship called the *Pearl,* was one of many seamen who got involved in smuggling fugitives out of slavery. In 1847, he sailed into Washington harbor with a cargo of oysters. At the dock, a black man asked him if he would be so kind as to take a woman and her five children north. The woman was a slave who had paid her owner for her freedom, said the man. But the slave owner refused to give her "free papers" and was threatening to send her to the dreaded deep South.

Captain Drayton allowed the woman, her five children, and her niece to stow away on board. Without any trouble, he took them

north, where the woman's husband was waiting for her. Thus, Drayton became a conductor on the secret, invisible Railroad that now stretched out over the ocean.

In 1848, he docked in Washington and prepared to take on a large group of runaway slaves. While the city celebrated the newly established Second Republic of France with speeches and a torchlight procession, slaves were left more or less to themselves. That is how so many of them—seventy-eight in all—were able to escape onto the *Pearl*, which sailed at midnight.

The ship reached the mouth of the Potomac River, and then the wind turned against it. Captain Drayton, his crew, and the hidden cargo had to hole up 150 miles from Washington.

The escape by then had been discovered and there was great excitement over the disappearance of seventy-eight slaves at one time. A steamer with armed men on board came after the *Pearl* and brought it back to Washington. An angry mob waited there to "greet" Captain Drayton and his crew.

All of the fugitives, worth more than $100,000 as property, were arrested. The male slaves were shackled by twos into a "coffle," a human train, and whipped through the streets. The female slaves followed behind. All were jailed as runaways. Fifty of them were sold to the local slave dealer to be auctioned.

Scores of indictments were brought against Captain Drayton and his crew. Two trials were held, and the accused were found guilty and given harsh sentences. They would remain in jail until the combined fines of $228,000 were paid.

Captain Drayton's own fine was $10,060, at the time a large amount that could cause him to be jailed for life. But four years later, Drayton's friends persuaded President Millard Fillmore to pardon Drayton and all of those in his crew who had been sentenced.

The slaves, however, were lost in the slave system. Sold and resold, they continued to labor and die, unless by some miracle they found a chance to run again.

As a result of the Drayton incident, slave-state representatives in Congress demanded a stronger Fugitive Slave Act.

Solomon Northup

Solomon Northup's father was given freedom through the legal will of his owner. Solomon was born free in 1808 in New York and grew up knowing next to nothing about slavery. He married and lived for a time in Saratoga, New York, where in the evenings he played his violin at social gatherings. By day, he worked in the hotels.

One day, Solomon met two men who were managers of a traveling circus. They asked him to join them as a musician. He agreed, and though he soon felt the managers acted oddly, he did stay on with the circus for a time.

One night, after a deep—possibly drugged—sleep, he woke up in a place called Williams' Slave Pen. This was a holding house for slaves and was in sight of the Capitol Building in Washington, D.C. The managers of the circus were also slave catchers of a particular kind. They were bounty hunters who received rewards of money from slave owners for capturing their runaway slaves. These bounty hunters were sometimes afraid to bring their cases to court under the Fugitive Slave Act of 1793. They feared that their often flimsy "proof" of ownership would not stand up. It didn't matter to them what black person they brought back, as long as the man, woman, or child fit a general description. The slave owner didn't care, either, and he would give the reward as soon as he got back a slave. The bounty hunters would watch a black person for a time, waiting for a chance to carry out their plan by trickery. Such was the unfortunate experience of the freeman Solomon Northup, in 1830.

Even though Solomon had never been a slave, he was handed over to a harsh slave owner in the South, Edwin Epps, and he became a slave laboring on the Epps plantation.

Years later Solomon wrote that he slept on "a plank twelve inches wide and ten feet long. My pillow was a stick of wood. The bedding was a coarse blanket, and not a rag or shred beside."

Though luck is rare in such cases, eventually Solomon Northup was lucky. A Northerner called Bass, who worked at the plantation, befriended Solomon and wrote to Northern friends about him.

The Bass letters reached Solomon's wife, Anne Northup, who petitioned the governor of New York. He in turn was concerned and interested enough to send an agent to find Solomon.

Citing the 1840 New York law against kidnapping, the governor's agent was able to get Solomon back to New York, even though Epps tried to prevent it. And in 1853, twenty-three years after he was kidnapped, Solomon Northup was finally free.

Frederick Augustus Washington Bailey

After his birth in 1817, Frederick Bailey was separated from his mother. He lived on a Maryland plantation with his grandmother. He had so little to eat as a child that he often had to fight the dogs in the yard—over bones with meat on them—so he wouldn't starve. He was eight years old when his owner sent him to Baltimore as a house servant for the family of Hugh Auld. Auld's wife broke the law by teaching Frederick to read and write. Her husband stopped her, saying that learning would only make the slave child unfit for slavery. He was right.

Auld died suddenly, and Frederick was sent back to the plantation as a field hand. Later on, when he was a young adult, a Sunday school he started was shut down by angry whites. He was beaten and flogged for resisting the slave system. He was even whipped every seven days for six months, to break his spirit. But Frederick Bailey's spirit would not be broken.

At sixteen, he was hired out on a ship. He and three other slaves plotted to escape but were found out before they could get away. Five years later, in 1838, Frederick disguised himself as a sailor and made good his escape. He found work as a laborer in New York City and then in New Bedford; Massachusetts. At that point Frederick Bailey changed his name to Frederick Douglass. Soon he would become the most renowned ex-slave of all time.

In 1841, now married, Frederick Douglass began talking about his experiences as a slave at meetings of antislavery societies. It wasn't long before he found his true calling as an orator and leader in the freedom crusade. His style and grace with words and his handsome appearance put him in the forefront of the movement. He became the lecturer for the Massachusetts Antislavery Society. He spoke across the country against slavery and straightforwardly told about his life as a slave to rapt listeners. But he was still a fugitive and he was always in danger of being recognized and caught as he traveled.

Not all the people who heard him were sympathetic to the cause of abolition. In Indiana, a white mob beat Douglass senseless and left him for dead. Yet he revived and went on recounting and denouncing the evils of slavery.

In 1845, he wrote an account of his life. Friends had asked him not to write it, fearing he would be found out as the runaway called Bailey. The biography was published and titled *Narrative of the Life of*

Frederick Douglass. Soon afterward, Douglass *was* recognized as Frederick Bailey and had to leave the country. He went to England, where he raised enough money from lecturing to buy his freedom. Two years later he returned to America a free man.

In 1847, Douglass started his own abolitionist newspaper, *The North Star.* It was dedicated to the cause of freedom for oppressed blacks. "It shall fearlessly assert your rights," he wrote in his first editorial, "faithfully proclaim your wrongs, and earnestly demand for you instant and even-handed justice. Giving no quarter to slavery at the South, it will hold no truce with oppressors at the North . . ."

Douglass's most famous speech came at a Fourth of July celebration in Rochester, New York, in 1852.

Fellow Citizens, pardon me, and allow me to ask, why am I called upon to speak here today? What have I or those I represent to do with your national independence . . . What to the American slave is your Fourth of July? I answer, a day that reveals to him more than all other days of the year, the gross injustice and cruelty to which he is the constant victim. To him your celebration is a sham . . . your sounds of rejoicing are empty and heartless . . . your shouts of liberty and equality, hollow mockery—a thin veil to cover up crimes which would disgrace a nation of savages . . .

Frederick Douglass was forced to flee to Canada when the governor of Virginia issued a warrant for his arrest, charging that he had conspired with abolitionist John Brown in the 1859 slave revolt at Harpers Ferry, Virginia.

Douglass did meet with John Brown, but only to advise him to

give up his plan. He strongly opposed it and was not a conspirator. John Brown was tried, convicted, and hanged in December 1859. Douglass stayed out of the country until the Virginia arrest warrant expired and the political climate in America had changed.

When the Civil War broke out in 1861, Douglass was certain that it would bring an end to slavery. He had two interviews with President Lincoln about recruiting black soldiers for the Union armies, an idea he strongly supported. Two of his own sons were the first recruits, and Douglass helped enlist the men of the celebrated 54th and 55th Massachusetts Negro regiments.

Douglass went on to write another biography, *Life and Times of Frederick Douglass*. He held public office as U.S. marshal of the District of Columbia, and then was named minister to Haiti.

On the day of his death, February 20, 1895, the North Carolina legislature held a day's adjournment in respect for his passing. He had been the leading black spokesman in America for half a century.

The Brave Conductor

She was called the greatest conductor on the Underground Railroad. Slaves named her Moses because, like the biblical Moses, she led her "travelers" from bondage to freedom. Araminta was the name given her, which she changed to Harriet after her mother. She was born into slavery in about 1820 in Dorchester County, Maryland, one of Harriet and Benjamin Ross's eleven children. As a slave child Harriet grew up with little time for play and no schooling. Instead, she had plenty of work and many beatings by her owner.

Sometime during her youth, Harriet Ross was hit on the head by a heavy weight thrown by her owner. The severe blow caused her to fall asleep whenever she was quiet for longer than fifteen minutes. She thus became physically active to keep herself awake.

As she grew older, Harriet did not often live with her owner; he hired her out to work for various people. This was a common practice in those times; when an owner no longer needed the services of one of his slaves, he rented the slave out to someone who did.

When she was in her twenties, word reached Harriet that she and two of her brothers were to be sold. She ran away, believing she had a right to liberty or death. "One or the other I mean to have," she said. She made a successful escape and found her way into free Pennsylvania.

Once free, Harriet stared at her hands to see if she was the same person out of slavery as she had been in it. She surely felt different. "There was such a glory over everything," she said. "The sun come like gold through the trees."

Unfortunately, Harriet had to leave behind her brothers and her husband, John Tubman, who had said he would report her if she ran.

Later she did go back for him, but he had already remarried. As John Tubman seeped out of her wounded heart, the woman known to history as Harriet Tubman devoted herself to the freeing of others.

She went about establishing a network of Underground stations from the South all the way into Canada, making more than twenty dangerous journeys into the South to do so.

She returned for her brothers and brought them out. She took her elderly mother and father north. Over her lifetime, Harriet Tubman brought out more than three hundred slaves along the Underground Railroad. Rewards for her capture, posted by the slave owners from whom she liberated slaves, finally reached the sum of $40,000. But

Harriet thought of everything. She hired someone to follow the man who posted descriptions of runaways. Once the man left the area, Harriet's assistant tore the posters down.

She carried a pistol at all times and a potion to quiet fugitive children if they began to cry. If the runaways she led were too fearful and wanted to turn back, she would point her pistol at them. "You go or you die," she would say. None ever died. "I never run my train off the track," said Harriet proudly.

Harriet Tubman became a heroine to the abolitionists. Northern antislavery leaders such as Thomas Garrett were always eager to help her with food, money, or lodging. She herself helped abolitionist John Brown (who called her General Tubman) in recruiting men for the uprising he led at Harpers Ferry.

In the 1850s, Harriet appeared at many antislavery meetings and also began speaking out on women's rights. Because of the huge price on her head, she was forced to flee to Canada just before the start of the Civil War. But she did return to America in 1862, and served as a spy, scout, and nurse for the Union Army in North Carolina.

After the war, she turned her home into the Home for Indigent and Aged Negroes, which supported freedpeople. She married Nelson Davis, a war veteran, in 1869.

Harriet Tubman lived out much of her old age in poverty. Then, thirty years after the Civil War's end, she received a war-widow's pension of $20 a month for the rest of her life. So humane was she that she used nearly all of the money to maintain her home, later known as the Harriet Tubman Home, as a refuge for the needy. She died in 1913, at the age of ninety-three.

"All Right, Sir!"

Henry Brown looked like an ordinary slave. That is, his owner never suspected him of wanting to run away. He thought Henry to be happily humble, slow to think and act, inferior in all ways.

But Henry was watchful and quick-witted, ever hopeful of finding a way to get himself gone from the Southern state of Virginia, which pressed close to the North. Although he had studied and studied the problem of escape, Henry Brown had hit upon no clear way. Yet he kept on thinking about the problem while he went about his daily chores on the plantation.

One day, in 1849, an idea struck him. Secretly, Brown had a box of his own design made. It was two feet eight inches deep, two feet wide, and three feet long. The box was lined with a soft yet sturdy feltlike fabric.

Henry's friend Samuel Smith, a carpenter, made the box for Henry. And when it was finished, Henry got inside it. There was not a large space inside, but he made himself as comfortable as he could. He had biscuits, a pouch of water, and a single tool, a gimlet, with a screw point at one end and a handle at the other. With the gimlet, Henry could bore holes in the wood so that he could breathe.

Samuel Smith nailed up Henry Brown's box with Henry inside. The box was circled with hickory hoops of the kind then used for crating.

It was addressed and marked THIS SIDE UP WITH CARE and taken to the Adams Express Company. Then it was transported by land on a horse-cart designed for carrying heavy loads, called a dray. It was handled and shifted at stops throughout the day and night. Expressmen were not too careful to place the box THIS SIDE UP. For hours, it seemed to Henry, he was situated on his head, the box being upside down.

Henry Brown was shipped from Richmond, Virginia, to Philadelphia, Pennsylvania, a box ride of some twenty-six hours. The box was expected in Philadelphia by a group of abolitionists. They had received a message that certain important "freight" was coming, and they were anxiously waiting.

Four of them were there to witness the grand opening when the box arrived at the antislavery office. One of the men was William Still, chairman of the Vigilance Committee of Philadelphia and the agent of the most important Underground Railroad station in Pennsylvania.

Later, Still would carefully write down Henry Brown's story, as he did the story of each fugitive who passed through his station.

The four abolitionists locked the office door and began the task of opening the "freight." One of them, Mr. McKim, tapped lightly on the box and called out, "All right?" He held his breath a second until the reply came from inside: "All right, sir!"

The four men said later that they would forever remember the moment. There was a saw at the ready. The men cut away the hickory hoops; they pulled out the nails and opened the lid.

Mr. Brown rose up from the box. He reached out to them and said, "How do you do, gentlemen?"

He was soaking wet with perspiration yet otherwise fine. He explained that he had told himself in Richmond that if he lived through the journey, he would sing a hymn. And this he did. It began, "I waited patiently for the Lord, and He heard my prayer."

It was a touching moment for all who witnessed it. Afterward, Henry Brown went on to Boston, where he was greeted as a hero. He stayed there and worked on the Underground Railroad, helping other fugitives. From then on, this former slave who had himself crated and shipped to freedom was known as Henry Box Brown.

Unfortunately, Henry Box Brown's carpenter friend Samuel Smith was not so lucky. He tried the same trick of escape with two more runaways. But he was betrayed. The fugitives were caught, and Smith went to prison for eight years.

PART THREE

EXODUS
TO FREEDOM

At the midpoint of the nine-teenth century, slaveholding planters believed that slavery was—or should be—a cornerstone of American life. The United States was one-half slave and one-half free, and the formal admission of California into the Union as a free state in 1850 would tip the balance against the slave states. Senator John C. Calhoun, of South Carolina, said the South would resist a free California, since it meant that free states would outnumber slave states. A movement for a convention, whose goal was the formation of a Southern confederacy, began.

To avoid a serious political conflict, President Zachary Taylor proposed that the Utah and New Mexico territories be organized to permit slavery at the same time that California was admitted as a free state. The president hoped this compromise would stop the South from working up the issue of secession, or withdrawal from the Union.

With other concessions added, including a second, harsher Fugitive Slave Act, the president's proposal was passed. Called the Compromise of 1850, it was meant to be a truce between slave states and free states and to put the slavery dispute to rest. But the truce brought no peace to anyone.

Northern abolitionists denounced the new Fugitive Slave Act. The need for it, they said, showed that slavery had never been secure in the South. Northerners flocked to the antislavery cause in large numbers, and thirteen Northern states passed personal liberty laws to thwart the new act. Ohio and New York courts stated that black people were free the moment they crossed the states' borders. Yet black people in the North felt increasingly threatened as the slave system and the new Fugitive Slave Act crept their way.

In the South, there was more talk of seceding from the Union. A shaky peace lasted until 1854, when Congress passed the Kansas-Nebraska Bill. This bill allowed Kansas and Nebraska to become territories that would decide their own slavery questions. In reality, it meant the territories were open to slaveholders.

Proslavery and antislavery settlers rushed to Kansas and clashed. Many people were killed; the territory became known as "Bleeding Kansas." The terrible strife that followed was one of the events leading to the outbreak of the Civil War in 1861.

Meanwhile, slaves still ran from the South, becoming fugitives from the slave system whenever they could. As conflict between the North and the South grew, the fugitives in effect ran right into the Civil War.

Anthony Burns

Anthony Burns was born a slave in 1834. He grew up as a favored slave child of his owner, John Suttle of Virginia. When Suttle died, his son Charles took over the maintenance of his father's slaves. Charles sold some slaves away in order to pay debts and began hiring Anthony Burns out.

Anthony was clever and brought in good money for his owner, so Charles Suttle also favored him. He even let Anthony arrange where he would work and what would be paid by the white men who hired him. Anthony often worked away from home and didn't see Suttle for weeks at a time.

As luck would have it, Anthony got a job near the Richmond docks in 1854. And it was here that he planned his escape. With the aid of a sailor friend, he hid aboard a ship bound for Boston, Massachusetts.

The hiding space was damp and dark, no better than a hole. It allowed Anthony to lie on one side, but it was so narrow that he could not turn. It was early spring, and Anthony had never known such cold weather. His feet half froze in his boots, and he became deathly ill from seasickness. The trip, which usually took ten days to two weeks, took almost three weeks.

"At the next port, put me off, please," Anthony begged his friend. "I cannot stand it any longer. Put me off the ship!"

But what about freedom? the sailor asked Anthony.

"It dies, because surely I am dying!" Anthony answered.

His friend assured Anthony that he would not die. He supplied Anthony with fresh water and bread and, once in a while, meat. When they docked in Boston, Anthony walked away limping, muscles aching, but a free man at last.

His freedom was short-lived. Charles Suttle, informed of Anthony's disappearance, had quickly discovered his whereabouts. He slipped into Boston and made arrangements for Anthony's capture.

One evening, as Anthony came home from work, he was set upon by a group of men, who arrested him and led him to the courthouse jail. There, Anthony was met by his owner.

Suttle bowed before Anthony. "How do you do, *Mistah* Burns!" he said with heavy sarcasm.

Later tried under the Fugitive Slave Act of 1850, Anthony Burns was defended by the leading abolitionist lawyers of the day. His capture in the North and his trial at the moment of the passage of the Kansas-Nebraska Bill were the last straw for antislavery people, who poured into Boston by the thousands to give Anthony Burns their support. Overzealous abolitionists even stormed the courthouse, but that failed to free Burns.

Despite the sympathy he aroused, Anthony Burns lost his case. He had recognized Suttle that fateful evening of his capture and had addressed Suttle as his owner. These facts were used against Anthony

by the prosecution, which was intent on upholding the Fugitive Slave Act.

Through streets thronged with thousands of citizens crying, "Shame! Shame!" and with hundreds of troops guarding him, Anthony Burns was marched to the docks and returned south by ship.

Again a slave, he was imprisoned and severely punished for a year. Each day, he was taken to the prison courtyard and exhibited like an animal. Indeed, he was called the Boston Lion by Southerners.

Eventually, his friends in Boston, led by the Reverend Leonard Grimes (himself a former slave), discovered Anthony's whereabouts and bought his liberty. Anthony Burns returned to Boston a hero and lectured widely on his treatment as a slave prisoner.

He moved to St. Catharines, Canada, and became the much-beloved minister of a congregation there. Yet the hardships he had suffered shortened his life. He died in July 1862.

Anthony Burns lived twenty-eight years, only nine of them as a free man. The life he lived would have defeated most men. Yet his was an important life. His case spurred the passage of the Massachusetts Personal Liberty Law on May 21, 1855. The law guaranteed that no individual could be arrested and jailed without first going before a judge or a court to decide whether the arrest had been justified.

After Anthony Burns, no fugitive from slavery was ever again taken back into bondage from the state of Massachusetts.

A Mother's Despair

Gone, gone,—sold and gone
To the rice-swamps dank and lone,
From Virginia's hills and waters,—
Woe is me, my stolen daughters!

This refrain comes from the poem "Farewell of a Virginia Slave Mother," by the renowned Quaker poet John Greenleaf Whittier. It expresses the outrage that abolitionists felt toward that most hateful feature of slavery, the breaking apart of slave families through their sale or auction. It was this tragic cutting away of mother from child and husband from wife that often pushed slaves to become fugitives.

Perhaps fearing just such a separation, Margaret Garner, her four children, her husband, Robert, and his parents, Simon and Mary, all attempted to run away from Boone County, Kentucky, in 1850. With nine other fugitives, they managed to cross the frozen Ohio River. Then, in Cincinnati, the group split up. Margaret and her family took refuge at the house of a black man they knew, a Mr. Kite.

They had been noticed, though, and before long the slaveholder and his posse were on their trail. All too soon, the posse came pounding at Kite's door and then broke in. Robert fired shots and wounded one of the posse, but he was overpowered and dragged away.

Margaret would rather see her children dead than as slaves again. By the time the posse reached her, she had taken a butcher knife and slit the throat of her favorite daughter. She would have taken the lives of the others if she'd had the time.

The group was placed in jail. Margaret was arrested for murder, and the others as her accomplices.

The public was stunned. Who was this woman who would kill her own child rather than see her remain a slave?

Margaret Garner was five feet tall and twenty-two years old, and was said to have keen, intelligent eyes. She was a mulatto. Her face was scarred on the forehead and cheekbone. As to the cause of the scars—"White man struck me" was all she would say.

She wore a turban in the courtroom and a dark calico dress. For all of the time of her trial, her two small boys played at her feet. She held her second little daughter, a child of about nine months, in her arms. Margaret's expression was forlorn and despairing, far beyond the reach of the words of cheer spoken by friendly abolitionists.

Margaret asked the judge to take her life. She would sing all the way to the gallows, she said. But he sent her back to slavery instead.

A quiet crowd followed Margaret and her family as they were escorted to the ferry. On the way back across the Ohio River to Kentucky, Margaret either jumped or fell overboard, with her smallest child in her arms. Men jumped in after her and saved her life. But the child was drowned. When Margaret heard this, she was overcome with

joy—yet another one of her offspring was out of the reach of bondage.

Soon afterward, Margaret Garner was said to be lost in "the seething hell of slavery." She was sold to the deep South, into the brutal, disease-ridden heat of the rice fields. Newspaper reports stated that she died of typhoid fever in 1858. Nothing was heard of her two small sons. Yet history remembers Margaret Garner—she with her will of steel, her fierce heart, and her love of family and freedom.

A Slave from Missouri

Dred Scott was born a slave in 1795, in Missouri. In 1834, when he was thirty-nine, he was bought as a house servant by Dr. John Emerson, an army surgeon. Emerson then moved with Dred Scott to the free state of Illinois. Later, they moved again to Fort Snelling, in the free territory of Wisconsin. There, Scott married Harriet and their first child was born.

When Dr. Emerson's work was finished at Fort Snelling, he brought Dred Scott and his family back with him to Missouri. Soon after that, Dr. Emerson died. And eight years later, Dred Scott got help from abolitionist lawyers. In 1847, he filed suit for his freedom in the Circuit Court of St. Louis, against Dr. Emerson's widow. Scott's grounds were that living in a free state and then a free territory had made him free.

For almost a decade, the Dred Scott lawsuit was a burning issue across America. The case, *Scott v. Sanford,* went to the Supreme Court. At the time, five justices out of nine were Southerners. Chief Justice Roger Taney was a Maryland slave owner. In his opinion, the Missouri Compromise* was unconstitutional, "Negroes" could not be regarded as citizens of the United States, and the Supreme Court could not deny the slaveholders' right to take their slaves anywhere in the North or in the South.

"It is the judgment of this court . . ." stated Taney, "that the plaintiff . . . is not a citizen of Missouri, in the sense in which that word is used in the Constitution . . ."

In other words, in the Court's opinion, Dred Scott was a person without civil rights. This was the United States Supreme Court's advocacy of slavery, said the abolitionists. The orator and former slave Frederick Douglass said that Chief Justice Taney could not "pluck the silvery star of liberty from our Northern sky."

Oddly enough, only weeks after the decision, Scott was set free by a new owner. Unfortunately, Dred Scott died a year later.

The Dred Scott decision of 1857 made slave owners more secure by strengthening proslavery forces. It appeared to give federal support

---

*Under the Compromise, Missouri entered the Union as a slave state, followed by Maine as a free state. Slavery was no longer permitted in the Louisiana territory. And by implication, slaves were also prohibited there.

to the idea that slavery was national and could be introduced into any United States territory.

It did great harm to the progress of African Americans in the United States by denying them citizenship and was not overturned for eleven years, until after the Civil War.

A Kentucky Runaway

It was in May 1857 that runaway Addison White was discovered living in the town of Mechanicsburg, Ohio. He'd been working there for about six months, trying to make enough money to bring his wife and children out of the South. When the United States deputy marshal for southern Ohio, with his posse of nine assistants, came looking for him, White took refuge in the attic of a house belonging to a man called Udney Hyde.

The marshal's posse fired on Hyde's house. Addison White fired back from the attic. As word spread of the incident, the people of Mechanicsburg rose up against the posse and the marshal. Men with

pitchforks and clubs, and women said to have the dough they'd been kneading still on their hands, chased the posse away. It returned two weeks later, only to hear that Addison White had long since taken the Railroad to Canada.

At that point, the marshal arrested citizens of the community for giving aid to a fugitive and helping him escape again.

Udney Hyde was an abolitionist who had sent over 500 fugitives along the Railroad, acting as the agent between two local Underground stations and stations forty miles to the northeast. Now he himself became a fugitive, hiding in the homes of his friends and in swamps. He knew he would go to prison if caught.

Angry citizens of Springfield and Xenia, Ohio, got out of bed to follow the posse as it headed south with the Mechanicsburg prisoners.

Meanwhile, Udney Hyde was still on the loose, still running. He knew the dark, winding country roads as well as he knew the backs of his hands and easily evaded those who sought him.

Members of the posse tried to capture Hyde when he sneaked home, but he disguised himself by covering himself with swamp mud. People who didn't recognize him laughed at the madman. People who knew him admired his cleverness.

The passage of time has clouded the events of the Addison White story. But his rescue had a lasting effect on the people of Ohio, making their opposition to slavery stronger than ever.*

---

*One hundred thirty-three years later, in 1990, members of the Ohio Historical Society and local advocates tried to save White's home in Mechanicsburg, Ohio, hoping to make it a historical landmark. But their efforts proved unsuccessful. New owners of the site bulldozed the house to make way for a parking lot.

Alexander Ross,
Down from Canada

Alexander Ross was a Canadian, a physician and a naturalist who wrote frequently about birds and insects. He knew the effects of slavery from seeing with his own eyes what it had done to fugitives in Canada, but reading *Uncle Tom's Cabin* spurred him to action. He came to the United States and sought out abolitionist Gerrit Smith. Smith in turn introduced him to distinguished radicals of the day. They all agreed that with his scientific knowledge, Ross might very well "invade" the South posing as a "muddled" professor. Under that cover, he could help the cause of freedom for slaves. And that is exactly what Alexander Ross did.

Because he was white and a gentleman, Ross could travel the South freely. He first went to Richmond, Virginia, to watch people and to learn. Before long, he talked to forty slaves at a preacher's house, telling them about routes north. These routes, he told the slaves, would take them along the Underground Railroad to safety. Ross gave the slaves names of people who would help them and directions to their towns. He also asked the slaves to pass the information on to other slaves who might want to run.

Word got around that a Northerner was in the area giving slaves directions for escape. Alexander Ross did even more than that. He provided another fugitive group with money, weapons, food, and a compass.

He quickly left the South for Pennsylvania before he could be captured. It was there that he developed a code for leading fugitives from one station on the Underground to the next.

In Ross's code, the number 29 was the town of Seville, Ohio. Medina, Ohio, was number 27. *Hope* was Cleveland and *sunrise* was Sandusky. *Midnight* was Detroit, Michigan. One can imagine one of Ross's messages: "We *hope* to rise at *sunrise;* then we will rest by *midnight*." The message marked the path of travel and the main towns where slaves would be helped on the Railroad.

Going to Canada, a fugitive might enter the country from *Glory to God,* Ross's code for Windsor, Ontario, or *God be Praised,* Port Stanley.

After a time Alexander Ross returned to the South. Under cover of his scientific field work, he moved from place to place, contacting slaves. No one ever realized that when slaves disappeared from one

plantation, "Professor" Ross was likely to be hunting rare insects in a field nearby!

Ross continued his secret work from the last years of the 1850s until the first guns sounded the beginning of the Civil War.

Jackson, of Alabama

Jackson was the slave of William R. King, of Alabama. King was elected vice-president of the United States in 1852, serving under President Franklin Pierce. While King was in Washington, Jackson ran away from the King home in Alabama to Cincinnati, Ohio.

Jackson was fairly safe there and it seemed that no one was looking for him. He knew how to cut hair, and he set up shop. He was successful at barbering for several years; everyone knew and liked Jackson.

But one day he was forcibly taken by a posse of men with bowie knives and pistols. Jackson fought and kicked and took heavy blows. A friend came to his aid, but the posse beat him off. It was noontime and most of the other shopkeepers were off to their meals; there seemed to be no police about. Jackson was forced onto the ferry to Covington, Kentucky. There, he was bound tightly and taken all the way back to Alabama, to slavery.

Sometime later Jackson met and courted a free Creole woman. Accounts as to how this came about are unclear (since he was once again a slave), but Jackson did marry this free woman of mixed black and Spanish or French ancestry. With her olive complexion and straight black hair she could easily pass for white. And when dressed in her finery, she looked quite the proper lady of the South.

Jackson and his wife thought of a plan. She would pose as a white woman of class on a trip to Baltimore. Jackson, who was small in stature, would disguise himself as her female servant.

They traveled this way on a boat to New Orleans without any trouble. Jackson's disguise worked perfectly.

When they reached New Orleans, they took another boat going to Cincinnati. And since there were several Southern ladies aboard, Jackson's wife ordered him about and he did her bidding as a proper servant would.

"But don't stop at Cincinnati," one Southern woman told Jackson's wife. "It is in a free state, you see. And the laws of the state make it that all slaves are free as soon as they touch its borders."

"Do stop at Covington, on the other side of the river," another lady said. "Leave your gal on the Kentucky side, where she is less likely to run away."

Haughtily, Jackson's wife explained that her servant was much too devoted to her to ever think of escaping. "She will not ever think to leave me," said the wife.

There were Northern ladies on the boat as well. They hastened to speak to Jackson (in disguise) privately when "her" owner was not too near.

"Seize the chance!" they told Jackson. "You are in a free state when we reach Cincinnati!"

Jackson merely shrugged. And the Northern women pitied this poor slave who was too devoted to try to escape.

The Southern "lady" with her "servant" took a carriage to a hotel run by a black man. Jackson knew the city well and had friends nearby. Once he and his wife were settled in the hotel, he sent one message to the abolitionist Levi Coffin and another to the Underground Railroad conductor John Hatfield. Both arrived at the hotel at about the same time and were directed to an upstairs parlor. There, the well-dressed Alabama lady greeted them. Her servant bowed politely. Then the lady asked Coffin and Hatfield for their advice. She said she wanted to free her servant and wondered if they could tell her how to proceed.

Levi Coffin wrote about what happened next:

The lady then ordered her servant to go into their bedroom and open her trunk and get out "that bundle." We supposed that she referred to some papers that she wished to show us . . . her servant returned, but the bundle seemed to be on the person, who had turned to a man. We recognized Jackson, the barber, at once, and greeted him with a hearty hand-shake. Then followed an introduction to his wife, a full explanation and a hearty laugh over the whole affair.

Jackson and his wife went on to Cleveland, where no one knew them. From there, he could easily cross over into Canada in case of danger. The couple settled down; Jackson opened a barbershop and soon had a thriving business. Never again was he troubled by slave catchers.

Wisdom

He was a slave and the only name he ever had was Wisdom. Wisdom ran away from Virginia. Some wagoners attached to the Union Army took him in and gave him work. However, Wisdom's owner was able to trace him and arrived at the Union camp to take him back. In the early days of the Civil War, it was not uncommon for Southerners to do that, under a "gentlemen's" truce by which they could regain their "property." At first, most Northern commanders cooperated, although reluctantly.

The Union officer of the day was Captain Swan. He didn't want to give Wisdom back into bondage and so took his time about locating the slave. "I don't know whether he is working in camp today or somewhere on the outskirts," he told Wisdom's owner.

Suspicious, the owner went to the camp's colonel, who ordered that the slave be brought forward. So it was that Wisdom was found. He was taken back to slavery by the owner and never heard from again. Even though the slave owner was required to show a certificate of slave ownership under the Fugitive Slave Act of 1850, Wisdom's owner did not. Such procedures were often ignored.

Nevertheless, the final hour of the Underground Railroad and fugitive slaves began with the Civil War: The Southern Confederacy

of 5 million whites and 3.5 million unhappy slaves was greatly out-numbered by the power of 20 million free people in the North.

Northerners, hearing about the Wisdom incident, were furious and frustrated. They made a crude dummy to represent the colonel and hung him in effigy.

An Unnamed Fugitive

As the Civil War continued, the situation for runaways improved. Slave owners left their plantations to fight for the Confederacy, and slaves began taking their chances with the Northern armies, where their free black brothers worked for pay. They escaped into the Union camps in ever-increasing numbers.

One such fugitive was employed as the servant of a Union major called Sherwood in a West Virginia regiment. In an effort to reclaim his slave, the fugitive's owner sent a marshal to Brigadier General Boyle of the Union Army. General Boyle in turn ordered Sherwood to return the slave to his owner.

Major Sherwood's reply was that he would give up his sword, but no fugitive slave would be returned south as long as he was in command. He was then arrested for disobeying an order. But before he could be court-martialed, the higher-ranking General Staunton revoked General Boyle's order. Major Sherwood never went to trial. In the meantime, the servant, hidden under an ambulance seat and taken out of the camp, finally reached safety in Canada.

Three Fugitives

One summer day in 1861, General Benjamin Butler, the Union commander of Fortress Monroe, in Virginia, found himself facing three runaway slaves. The fugitives told General Butler that their owner had joined the Confederate Army and had ordered them to go to North Carolina to build fortifications for the Confederacy. Instead, they had run to Fortress Monroe.

General Butler didn't know why he should send these former slaves away when he needed laborers himself. So he set them to work for him.

It wasn't long before the slave owner's agent came into the camp looking for the runaways.

Butler saw that slave labor was power to the Confederacy, for it allowed the owners to fight in the war. And he told the slave agent, "I will keep these three as contraband."*

As word got around about the sympathetic Butler, "contraband" began arriving at the fortress day after day. In a month, a thousand men, women, and children were there, ready and able. By July 1861, freedom was given to fugitives coming behind Union lines. Another order soon gave them wages.

In August, Butler's decision to seize the "contraband" became army policy when Congress passed the Confiscation Act. The act freed slaves of so-called masters at war with the Union.

---

*Contraband, or goods meant for the enemy that had been seized, became a popular code word in the North for fugitive slaves. The word was first used this way by General Butler.

Exodus

In 1862, the Northern states seemed to be filled with stops on the Underground Railroad. There was a war going on, and the Railroad's great cause was to get as many slaves as possible far out of bondage. There were now twice as many helpers on the Railroad as there had been only a few years before.

"Property" in slaves worth $1 million was lost every week from South Carolina alone. Other Southern states also complained that they were losing millions in "property." Slaves melted away from Missouri, Kentucky, and Tennessee into Kansas, Iowa, and Illinois. They vanished, then reappeared on the Union side, half clothed, half starved. And they kept coming.

Border-state slaves simply put down their plows, their serving trays, their horse-and-buggy reins. They grabbed the children and they left. If ever they did labor again as the war carried on, it would be with the Union armies, to plant fields for the soldiers and themselves.

This was a great leave-taking, confusing and tumultuous, not unlike the Exodus in which the Israelites left Egypt with Moses as their leader. The blacks had the north star of freedom to lead them and the ever-present Union armies to lean upon. But the slave exodus was also a burdensome number of men, women, and children to be housed, fed, and clothed. In truth, it was a revolution, as 500,000 oppressed people full of hope left the slave fields and all areas of their unpaid labor. They flowed into the Union camps in search of freedom. They were a treasure ready to be spent on winning for the North.

General Benjamin Butler called for black freemen—200,000 still lived in the South—to defend the Union.

Frederick Douglass called for black regiments to help.

Abolitionists called for President Lincoln to free all slaves.

In April 1862, Congress freed slaves in the District of Columbia. It paid their owners as much as $300 for each one freed. In June 1862, Congress abolished slavery in all territories.* Lincoln issued the Emancipation Proclamation in preliminary form in September 1862. He then warned the South that it must return to the Union or in one

---

*These were regions of the United States that were not yet states but had their own legislature and officers, appointed by the president.

hundred days, on the first of January 1863, all persons held as slaves in the rebellious states would go free. The South did not return to the Union, and on the given date the final Proclamation was issued.

A Proclamation

The Emancipation Proclamation was drafted in 1862 and put into effect on January 1, 1863. It freed about a million slaves in the states and parts of states that had seceded from the Union and were in rebellion. It exempted Tennessee and parishes around New Orleans because they were then considered under federal government control.*

---

*Some 3 million slaves in states bordering on the North and *not* in rebellion (Missouri, Kentucky, and counties of western Virginia, Maryland, and Delaware) were not affected by the Proclamation and were not yet free.

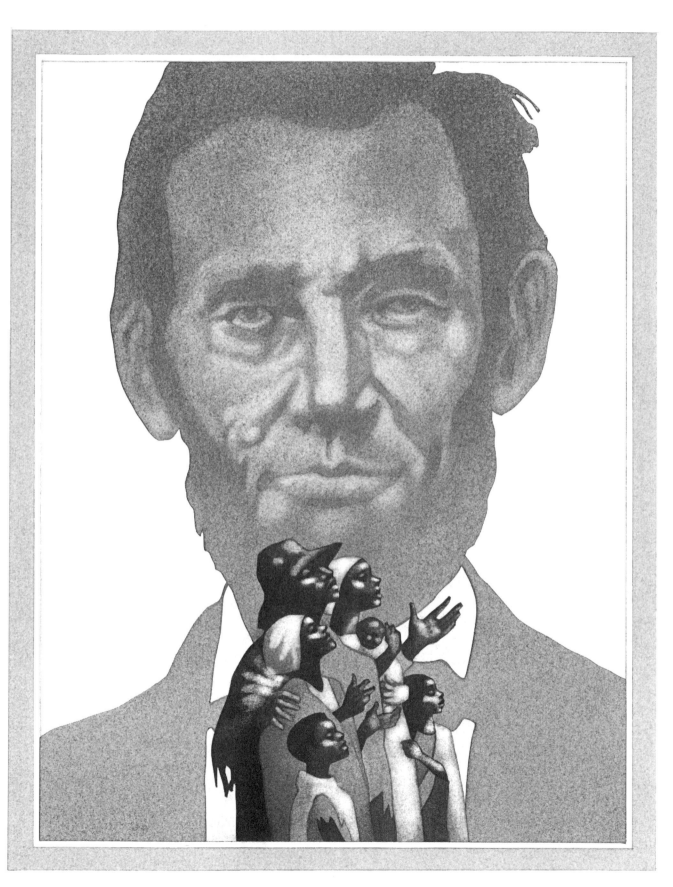

Now, therefore, I, Abraham Lincoln, President of the United States, by virtue of the power in me vested as Commander-in-Chief of the Army and Navy . . . in time of actual armed rebellion against the authority and government of the United States, and as a fit and necessary war measure for suppressing said rebellion, do, on this 1st day of January, A.D. 1863 . . . order and designate as the States and parts of States wherein the people thereof . . . are this day in rebellion against the United States the following, to wit:

Arkansas, Texas, Louisiana . . . Mississippi, Alabama, Florida, Georgia, South Carolina, North Carolina, and Virginia (except the forty-eight counties designated as West Virginia . . .).

. . . I do order and declare that all persons held as slaves within the said designated States and parts of States are, and henceforward shall be, free; and that the Executive Government of the United States, including the military and naval authorities thereof, will recognize and maintain the freedom of said persons.

And I hereby enjoin the people so declared to be free to abstain from all violence, unless in necessary self-defense; and I recommend to them that, in all cases when allowed, they labor faithfully for reasonable wages.

And I further declare and make known that such persons of suitable condition will be received into the armed service of the United States to garrison forts, positions, stations and other places, and to man vessels of all sorts in said service.

And upon this act, sincerely believed to be an act of justice, warranted by the Constitution upon military necessity, I invoke the considerate judgement of mankind and the gracious favor of Almighty God.

Abraham Lincoln

Deliverance

Jubilee was the term most slaves used for emancipation. Frederick Douglass was in Boston's Tremont Temple with hundreds of black and white abolitionists on New Year's Day, 1863. He waited for the message that would tell them that Lincoln had indeed issued the Proclamation. When it came, the packed church audience shouted and cried out, rising to sing the anthem: "Sound the loud timbrel o'er Egypt's dark sea, Jehovah hath triumphed, his people are free."

The account below is taken from the autobiography of Jacob Stroyer, a South Carolina slave who was freed by the Emancipation Proclamation:

Hark! I hear the clanking of the ploughman's chains in the fields; I hear the tramping of the feet of the hoe-hands. I hear the coarse and harsh voice of the Negro driver [he who worked directing field task gangs] and the shrill voice of the white overseer swearing at the slaves. I hear the swash of the lash upon the backs of the unfortunates; I hear them crying for mercy from the merciless. Amidst these cruelties I hear the fathers and mothers pour out their souls in prayer,—"O, Lord, how long!" and their cries not only awaken the sympathy of their white brothers and sisters of the North, but also mightily trouble the slave masters of the South.

. . . At last came freedom. And what joy it brought! I am now standing, in imagination, on a high place just outside the city of Columbia in the spring of 1865. The stars and stripes float in the air. The sun is just making its appearance from behind the hills, and throwing its beautiful light upon green bush and tree. The mocking birds and jay birds sing this morning more sweetly than ever before. Beneath the flag of liberty there is congregated a perfect network of the emancipated slaves from the different plantations, their swarthy faces, from a distance, looking like the smooth water of a black sea. Their voices, like distant thunder, rend the air,—"Old master gone away, and the Negroes all at home, There must be now the kingdom come and the year of jubilee."

The old men and women, bent over by reason of age and servitude, bound from their staves [threw aside their staffs], praising God for deliverance.

The Tide of Freedom

Representatives of the Union Army read the official word of emancipation to black and white Southerners by the thousands. The Southerners came to listen on street corners in towns, on plantations, in churches, in schools, and in farmyards across the Southern states. Sometimes a slave owner would give the news to his slaves.

There were jubilee celebrations throughout America as word moved along the Underground grapevine. Slaves did not hear about the coming of freedom all on the same day or at the same time (in Texas, emancipation came to be known as Juneteenth—June nineteenth—the celebration day former Texas slaves designated to symbolize jubilee for all of them). Moreover, the majority of the 4 million black people in

the United States would remain enslaved until the ratification of the Thirteenth Amendment to the Constitution, in December 1865.

In 1863, the Union boldly enlisted black soldiers, thus making extraordinarily good use of former slaves. In all, some 200,000 American blacks served in the Union's military. They would participate in twenty-nine major battles, including Richmond and Appomattox. Sixteen of them would receive the Congressional Medal of Honor. When they marched to war they sang "No More Auction Block for Me," the joyous anthem of freedom written by some nameless, inspired former slave, most likely in the year of jubilee:

> No more auction block for me,
>   No more, no more!
> No more auction block for me;
>   Many thousand gone.
>
> No more driver's lash for me,
>   No more, no more!
> No more driver's lash for me;
>   Many thousand gone . . .

Afterword

With the ratification of the Thirteenth Amendment to the Constitution on December 18, 1865, there was freedom, finally, for all of the 4 million African Americans. There would be no more bondage, no more running away. Slavery was abolished in America. And never had humankind seen freedom given at once to so many.

What do you do with freedom? the freed people wondered. But when they had time of their own to think about it, they knew. Some thought they would own the land of their former so-called masters. Many of the great Southern mansions now stood deserted. The slave-quarter cabins were largely empty as well.

Who would defend the freed once the Union armies left the former land of the Confederacy? Only a quarter of the slaves had safely reached the Union lines before the end of the war. The rest of the freed remained in the former land of slavery, a dark, despised reminder to the South of its defeat.

The blacks knew they would have to learn to defend themselves. They went away down the roads, as they had been doing for years, and to the forests. But now they did not run away. Now they were free to have nothing but the Southern roadside. They were free to have rain soak them day and night as they lay unsheltered. Nothing had ever come easy for them. And liberty would not come without hardship. If they ran now, it was only from disease and starvation, and from the race haters.

Help came in 1865, with the formation of the Freedmen's Bureau (1865–1872), which provided health and educational services for former slaves, in addition to provisions, fuel, and shelter. The bureau also administered all lands abandoned in the South. It could assign to every male freedman or refugee (a white male) up to forty acres of land.

However, that same year President Andrew Johnson restored most abandoned land in the South to its former owners, leaving little left for distribution. In 1866, he vetoed a bill to establish a permanent bureau. Thus, though it did provide food and clothing and help establish black colleges, public schools, and hospitals, the bureau did not bring any lasting economic security to former slaves. The great scholar and educator Dr. W. E. B. Du Bois called the Freedmen's Bureau the "most extraordinary and far-reaching institution of social uplift that America has ever attempted." He also called it a splendid failure.

In 1866, the Civil Rights Acts were passed, giving African Americans citizenship and protecting them from oppressive laws and codes.

After the Civil War, African Americans were able to find the best in life. They were free to seek education and to found their own universities. They were free to find jobs, to live together in families, to own land, to farm, to make homes, to cook and clean for themselves, to raise babies that were their own, to paint, to write, to sing, to read. And they were free to defend themselves as, increasingly, attempts were made to reenslave them.

They did all of these things almost as soon as the war was over. For 125 years they have continued to do so.

Virginia Hamilton

Yellow Springs, Ohio
March 1993

BIBLIOGRAPHY AND USEFUL SOURCES

Adams, Russell L. *Great Negroes Past and Present*. Chicago: Afro-Am Publishing Company, 1963.

Aptheker, Herbert, ed. *A Documentary History of the Negro People in the United States*, Vol. I. New York: Citadel Press, 1951.

——— *American Slave Revolts*. New York: Columbia University Press, 1943.

Bennett, Lerone, Jr. *Before the Mayflower: A History of Black America*. Chicago: Johnson, 1982.

Blockson, Charles L., ed. *The Underground Railroad*. New York: Prentice Hall Press, div. of Simon and Schuster, 1987.

Botkin, B. A., ed. *Lay My Burden Down: A Folk History of Slavery*. Chicago: University of Chicago Press, 1945.

Buckmaster, Henrietta. *Let My People Go*. New York: Harper & Brothers, 1941.

Cain, Alfred E., ed. *The Winding Road to Freedom: A Documentary Survey of Negro Experiences in America*. Yonkers, N.Y.: Education Heritage, 1965.

Carman, Harry J., and Harold C. Syrett. *A History of the American People*, Vol. I, to 1865. New York: Alfred A. Knopf, 1952.

Coffin, Levi. *Reminiscences*. Cincinnati: Western Tract Society, 1876.

Drayton, Daniel. *Personal Memoirs*. Boston: B. Marsh, 1855.

Du Bois, W. E. B. *Black Reconstruction in America, 1860–1880*. New York: Harcourt, Brace, 1935.

——— *The Suppression of the African Slave-Trade to the United States of America, 1638–1870*. New York: Schocken, 1969. (First published in 1896.)

Educational Research Council of America, Social Science Staff. *The American Adventure*, Vol. I. Boston: Allyn and Bacon, 1975.

Hammon, B., J. A. U. Gronniosaw, P. Wheatley, J. Hammon, and A. Jones. Slave narratives combined in one volume. Wiesbaden, Germany: Kraus Reprint Nendeln Lessingdruckerei, 1972. J. A. U. Gronniosaw. "A Narrative of the Most Remarkable Particulars in the Life of James Albert Ukawsaw Gronniosaw, an African Prince—Related by Himself." London: R. Groombridge, Panyer-Alley, Paternoster-Row, 1840.

Henson, Josiah. *Father Henson's Story of His Own Life*. Boston: John P. Jewett, 1858. (First published as *The Life of Josiah Henson*. Republished by Literature House, imprint of the Gregg Press, Upper Saddle River, N.J., 1970.)

Jacobs, Harriet Brent, *Incidents in the Life of a Slave Girl, Written by Herself*, ed. L. Maria Child. Miami: Mnemosyne Publishing Co., c. 1969 (reprint). (Boston: Published for the author, L. Maria Child, c. 1860).

McDougall, Marion Gleason. *Fugitive Slaves: 1619–1865*. Boston: Ginn and Company, 1891.

Miller, Randall, and John Davi Smith, eds. *Dictionary of Afro-American Slavery*. Westport, Conn.: Greenwood Press, 1988.

Morison, Samuel E., Henry S. Commager, and Wm. Leuchtenburg. *The Growth of the American Republic,* Vol. I. London: Oxford University Press, 1969.

Morris, Richard B. *Encyclopedia of American History*. New York: Harper & Brothers, 1953.

Perdue, Charles L., Jr., Thomas Barden, and Robert K. Phillips, compilers and eds. *Weevils in the Wheat: Interviews with Virginia Ex-Slaves,* "Interviews Conducted by the Virginia Federal Writers' Project in 1936–41." Charlottesville, Va.: University Press of Virginia, c. 1976.

Ploski, Harry A., and Roscoe C. Brown, compilers and eds. *The Negro Almanac*. New York: Bellwether, 1967.

Quarles, Benjamin. *Black Abolitionists*. London: Oxford University Press, 1969.

Seibert, Wilbur H. *The Underground Railroad from Slavery to Freedom*. New York: Macmillan, 1898.

Sloan, Irving J., compiler and ed. *Blacks in America, 1492–1970*. Dobbs Ferry, N.Y.: Oceana, 1971.

Spradling, Mary Mace, ed. *In Black and White,* Vols. I and II and supplement. Michigan: Gale Research, 1980.

Still, William. *Underground Railroad Records*. Philadelphia: Porter & Coates, 1862.

Stroyer, Jacob. *My Life in the South*. Salem, Mass.: Newcomb & Gauss, 1898. (c. 1879, entered according to Act of Congress by Jacob Stroyer, in the office of the Librarian of Congress at Washington, D.C. Reprinted by Arno Press and *The New York Times,* 1968, in *Five Slave Narratives,* Wm. Katz, ed.)

Truth, Sojourner. *Narrative of Sojourner Truth: A Bondswoman of Olden Time, Drawn from Her "Book of Life."* Boston: Published for the Author, 1875.

Wilson, Henry. *History of the Rise and Fall of the Slave Power in America*. Boston: J. R. Osgood & Co., 1872.

INDEX